petals of zero
petals of one

petals of zero petals of one

a n d r e w   z a w a c k i

Talisman House, Publishers

2009 • Jersey City • NJ

Published in the United States of America by
Talisman House, Publishers
P.O. Box 3157
Jersey City, New Jersey 07303-3157

ISBN: 978-1-58498-064-3

for Brian Henry

amitié pour l'exigence d'écrire
qui exclut toute amitié

Contents

The wires in the rose are beautiful

Jack Spicer

GEORGIA

I don't sleep Georgia

I shoot bullets into the dark

the blunt mimeographic dark

the middle dark Georgia

outside the outside

whatever a ghost's front tooth is Georgia

let alone ballistics

whatever pulls back the hammer Georgia

coughing up sulfur and strobes of negate

I wait Georgia

think Georgia

the fire is like the snow Georgia

the snow wipes out a oneway street puts nothing in its place

snow is not like the snow Georgia

one is theorem the other will thaw

night is the neighbor girl

she hangs her laundry

she sits on the step

the leaves on the tree in her yard are like florins

her sliding door dress in a squall Georgia

her flowers what is a flower Georgia

a trace what is trace

I listen to the noises every last one Georgia

I love every last noise on the violet fields

they bicker and click

the clamors I mean

blur as if struck with a Lucifer match

guesswork Georgia

netherlight's joke

I see smoke it rises it quadrilles Georgia

tungsten Georgia

sliver tongued

the smoke is a little less smoke in the air

little by little Georgia

it comes to that

not even Georgia

I walk wolfstep into the shadow Georgia

the nodding orchestral branches

shellacked as if a fountain turned and forced its gravity turn

the skuzzy drag queen dawn Georgia

hours away from hours away

a motor idles

reverse in the drive

tromp-l'œil frisking the shrubbery Georgia

the high beams taper the porch lamp expires

I take out the garbage Georgia

will it rain or snow

will the weather Georgia

the winter here is not your winter

it's pixeled it's *chien et loup* Georgia

a dumdum blank to the clavicle Georgia

assassin crouched at the front of the house assassin waiting in back

I don't give a shit Georgia

difference itself can differ Georgia

and everything's different now

I buried a friend far away Georgia

in France Georgia

it wasn't funny Georgia

we sat at a table I kissed him goodbye he turned around never came back

maybe you already heard it Georgia

I'm tired of talking about it

that was then and this is then and not even Georgia not even

I listen Georgia

to the racket the clatter

the clangors clang if you hearken Georgia

and that noise makes a noise if you

a peloton of din Georgia

you have to sonar yourself

The question of is is is it Georgia

the ranges are thrift store crinoline Georgia

the stars are of mescal

casbahs of tin

flayed what is it to flay something Georgia

mountains unplugged the moon flipped off

if music is cleaved from a flower Georgia

if music cleaves to the flower Georgia

liveforever and purple clover

but nothing lives that long Georgia

or even half that long .

All things that are are unlit Georgia

black like lapis in a quitted room

the feedback Georgia

the anvil's hymnal

a dial-tone looped in a flophouse Georgia

an explosive packed in a microchip

petals of 0 petals of 1

rips a hole of a fractal dimension

shrapnel Georgia

collateral damage

call it what you will

Here is the road the outskirts Georgia

here is a city

is the same city

and I don't know this city Georgia

and I don't know if I want to know

what is it that anyone knows Georgia

really Georgia

in the end Georgia

Some say your eyes are charcoal Georgia

some say siren some djinn

I don't say Georgia

it isn't for me

I don't have a bone in my body

the unquick have a habit of loitering Georgia

a bad one I willn't say otherwise

it seems to get them through alright

don't know what they see in it

as if they're awake what is wakefulness Georgia

with the silencer on what is silence Georgia

someone around here will know Georgia

somebody ought to know something

The house next door has gone tattletale gray

its chimney a jigsaw of mortar and frost

threadbare nay barren

crash tested Georgia

rapunzeling up on a fidgety draft

the pine straw to flicker and parry

and the eglantine to wither Georgia

and snowflakes tatter the shutters Georgia

like flak from a showdown in Kelvin air

"*L'attente commence quand il n'y a...*" Georgia

"*...plus rien à attendre, ni même la fin de l'attente*"

that nothing come between us Georgia

but me

and you

and the hollow between

I prune your buds

unbutton my ribs

pot you inside like a bonsai Georgia

buddha napping in tiny shade

buddha at rest with an almsgiving bowl

it's aliment vs. ailment Georgia

I won't let you go it alone

you and your poor man's briar patch

and your ne'er-do-well well well

Heat lightning daubs the collodion hills

and a howling

and how close

how close to the bone does it get Georgia

do you pull its pin with a cinch of the jaw

pulver its craw with a flinch of the fist

I hurry here is the wind

and cold the inaudible decibel

the irises flushed in saffron

in bayonet red

in cymbeline

no clean angle

simulacra Georgia

everything's dirty and doubled Georgia

I say

you can try to break it it will break you

I say

everything is breakable Georgia

melody Georgia

melt water

a pressure a femur a fever a wife

syllables virused by syllables Georgia

the bicycle is

the memory card is

the brackish canal where a boat is Georgia

and the boat and where is it headed Georgia

the tanzanite dew of your nerve endings

cuts me keeps me alert

I unlatch the window

it sticks Georgia

sometimes I see past the paint flecks Georgia

and sometimes the pane is the object I see

and sometime come a whirring Georgia

like an alabaster lung Georgia

a valentine stitched in Kevlar Georgia

blown in Venetian glass

it's beautiful Georgia

that's one word

like a landslide

like a negligée

carnelian Georgia

an impasse's path

the glass in the garden is bulletproof

but our bodies are not of glass Georgia

let's bloom Georgia

this popstand

this podunk five and dime a dozen

our brains all over the passenger seat

our underwear on the dash

desire from the formal idea thereof

I

is a shotgun shell Georgia

imma- and imminent

the image as such

your quidditas throws a wrench in the work

but this engine runs on wrenches Georgia

anti-freeze and no egress Georgia

parousia stalled in a parking lot

the phenomenon's faulty ignition

you're alasless Georgia

harassless Georgia

from your slackass jeans to your Jesus Georgia

ersatz and aliased

lacking alack

sans any essence or pretense of presence

you're leeward Georgia

a bejeweled word Georgia

and fuck you anyway

vowellewd Georgia

face card missing a face Georgia

they're dead Georgia

I said they were dead

I didn't say they weren't dancing

The clouds are low they will tumble down Georgia

I spread my arms they get tired Georgia

to catch them Georgia

from shattering Georgia

my eyes they get tired I don't shut them Georgia

it's like this Georgia

unlike this Georgia

between the bed and the kitchen Georgia

one plate and another

one fag and another

the ashtray the butane lighter Georgia

an ice cube and its plastic cell

a pill and the pillow

whetstone and knife

one bag of coffee one packet of creamer an orange a slice of bread

between the door and the hinge Georgia

the razor blades and the bathtub Georgia

a forest of goneness a windrow of kindling a forge nail hidden in grass

I don't cry Georgia

you know what they say

whoever the they is who say what they say

but I was never real Georgia

but the hell if I know what is

I'm a scarecrow Georgia

a voodoo doll

no for a left leg yes yes for my right it's calamity Georgia

flammable Georgia

periplum scribbled all over the board

a torso of origami folds

crease for an eyelash a Crayola head

with a watermark Georgia

80-gram

you roll it you lick it you drag on it Georgia

I don't say it ain't kitschy Georgia

like cotton candy

like holding hands

so you've had it up to here huh

there isn't a soul who don't have it to here

the android floral in cyanine Georgia

acacia version 2.0

the horizon a linen of spilled anjou

of lint and candle wax

I call Georgia

my voice shot Georgia

parasites sur la ligne Georgia

the flowers rattle

I 'listen the flowers'

and the I I am is that ruckus Georgia

it's pretty Georgia

that's a word comes to mind

a punkass word

but a word all the same

an adjective out of bric-a-brac

we let it return to its querulous hive

"a heaven of stones whose / swiftness..." Georgia

"...made their separate orbits / one, that slackening would fall"

I call out Georgia

because that you

because that you are whatever Georgia

but it's dint Georgia

Teflon Georgia

polycarbonate it opens on impact Georgia

beryl raised to the second power with the safety off and the trigger rigged

I don't knock Georgia

my brass knuckles buffed

with a rough like liquid oxygen and a pilot light and a fraying fuse

it's sugar Georgia

burnt Georgia

pure cane Georgia and maybe baby you're

nothing more than synecdoche Georgia

a piece of a shred of a shard of a frag-

you're blitzkrieg Georgia

don't 'lady' me Georgia

I've got theremin lacing the bloodstream George

and a spinning roulette for a ticker George

a slug cocked snug in the six-shooter chamber

a 16.6% chance

You're a bitch Georgia

a drill bit

by me I mean third-person plural Georgia

a lake effect Georgia

all haggardlike Georgia

a hangman Georgia

a hanged man Georgia

here's a lullaby Georgia

with geraniums Georgia

there there Georgia

no there there Georgia

and may your dreams be couturier sewn

in pinafores and dainty furbelow

It's not the same midnight threnody

that 3 in the morning laments

an asthmatic wheeze in the lavender Georgia

a powwow of bats in the arbor Georgia

aurora borealis Georgia

haint blue

and barleycorn bluish and pollen do powder the sill Georgia

'n' still Georgia

"The first snow was a white sand

that made the white rocks seem red"

hence I wed Georgia

the roof with the ladder

lean out to inquire of the distance

there's a lot to be learned by leaning Georgia

I can't put a number to it

nothing that matters is numbered Georgia

if anything can truly be said to

plaster cast and splint Georgia

weeds that whisker a cracking quoin

lachryma Georgia

the spigot leaking

laid thee down by the waters and wept

the driveway tailored in crepe Georgia

I swept it of leaves the leaves didn't stay

I swept it of bluster the gust did not stay

my scarce understanding of oak didn't stay

nor knowledge of climate

nor knowledge of season

dampness didn't

and dryness didn't

and I didn't stay there myself Georgia

any old thing can unsolder a moment

nearly everything does

erosion is a simple name for it Georgia

but it hides other themes that are hard

like a noun it takes the place of a thing

but doesn't kill it off

it shackles the signified to a stump

then chucks the log in the crick

a façade Georgia

a fusillade

the firing squad and the wall Georgia

a cenotaph

in the aftermath

of petty Georgia

your petticoat slipping

pussy- and pistolwhipped son of a Georgia

if I ever

I swear if I

if you ever so much as hint at Georgia

I don't know what I'd fixin' to fix ya

know not what I would do

but no one's ever sure what they're capable of

so I try Georgia

I try to remit

this dragnet that dredges the ends of an earth

what is it Georgia

is it Georgia

or is it not

I can't figure it Georgia

'twon't stay in focus

it doesn't possess a center or an outside

or an in

I'd say

like skipping a stone and the shale doesn't sink

or taming a tidal wave with a riding crop

or swimming inside a prism Georgia

its J/psi particles and xanadus of jade

bladed among the tall vitrines of a gilt arcade in a country Georgia

fenestral Georgia

and fractured Georgia

and can't tell where your skin leaves off and the color begins to begin

like looking for midday at 2 of the

clock when your 5 o'clock

shadow is early

but truth is it isn't like anything Georgia

not like any anything

not even currents are so much surrounded

they can't be split one from the water

you can call it a fact of life if you like

but it's nothing to do with facticity Georgia

let alone with a life Georgia

let alone with someone else's life

I don't know Georgia

don't know what I don't

sleet the drizzle the banshee oblique

high-volt deadbolt barbwirespeak

and I'm damned if you do either Georgia

the both of us are damnation Georgia

a hawk owl perched on the larch's bough

and rot

"But a sudden piece of glass on a sidewalk" Georgia

"Or a nickel tune in a music box

A shadow on a wall at night

And I would remember"

or December beneath a kaleidoscope rain

a digital rain

la pluie numérique

a lukewarm rinse without downpour Georgia

velocity Georgia

lovely as luck

that shower kick up as a rustle Georgia

a madrigal solo

a hiss in the cedars

some scrape from out back like flintlock Georgia

on the wood pile

on the axe handle

dithers and zags like a swarm Georgia

dilly-

dally and para-

diddle

a gramophone needle's static Georgia

on the asphalt Georgia

the police station roof

a wet from up north in a weight from up north

like a secret swerving toward rumor Georgia

it lapses Georgia

collapses Georgia

and the shush it starts to divide Georgia

by square root

by willow root

it fractions in Fibonacci Georgia

like artillery Georgia

like friendly fire

by logarithm by analog

it unloads Georgia

the cargo it's schlepped

renders its ballast elastic Georgia

dilates Georgia

dilutes itself

flutes the ravine and the river gap Georgia

letterpressed Georgia

an accordion's chord

like the soggy crumbs of Hop o' My Thumb

or HTML from the stratosphere Georgia

in smithereens Georgia

alarm tripped Georgia

out the emergency exit marked Georgia

I draw a line in the gravelly sand

you draw a break in the line

it's not right Georgia

quasi-floozy

a kite panhandling the breeze Georgia

pinned to the sky like a wedding corsage

on a tie-dye concert tee

The trees stand gunmetal

steel in the storm

then crack like a rifle report

nobody sees it coming Georgia

at crepuscule

in the alkaline dusk

maybe that's half the excitement Georgia

you would know better

bitterer than I

my opium Georgia

with your feldsparring drawl

my slapstick and lipstick and stick 'em up Georgia

you twang Georgia

like a daisycutter

a radio transmitter's muttering dreck

I'm an echo playing bumper cars in basilicas of Georgia Georgia

a silhouette

I'm a satin flower

I'm a sick bag and the sick Georgia

an avalanche an insomniateque

a ruby-throated humming

from my throat if I had a throat Georgia

it's not unlike a kiddie cartoon

fluorescent way out of proportion Georgia

I see horses

running through diamonds Georgia I

can't hold

it all in my head

it's sad Georgia

like the word itself

I hesitate to use it

but sometimes another word won't do when a word is the one you want

you think Pierrot Georgia

like pirouette Georgia

dunno if the words are related

I know almost nothing of language Georgia

I care too much to care

I lie down on the couch

a few birds a small tremor

the wind is encoded to rustle the gowns of the trees

a chirp like spit bite acid Georgia

an injection Georgia

an infection Georgia

via authorized medical application of a sterilized syringe

I went

too far Georgia

not near far enough

like a switch on the fritz in a binary star

and the steering column is hotwired Georgia

and piss in the tank for petrol Georgia

listing hydraulic or limping on fumes

to seize the shore of your flash flooded cellar

before it unfastens the linoleum floor

I'm sorry Georgia

I'm not sorry Georgia

I don't mean a single word that issue forth from mine own mouth

"what lies / outside us…" Georgia "…is not formless, it's

as we are, the sound itself"

I've heard Georgia

on entering an unfamiliar room

a blind person locates the source of that sound

leaky faucet

a failing bulb

the refrigerator's drone

and orients her touch around this point

sometimes the sound is a second person

in which case community Georgia

at others the ear meets no obstacle

and one is unmoored in a dumbshow of one

overhearing the blood move around in the brain

centrifugal Georgia

inch by inch

the fulcrum permits a perimeter Georgia

like rings advancing radaresque in a pond where a pebble

snapped the surface

curve by corner by

lintel by latch

then ricochet Georgia

like noon off a gun

the exterior turns internal Georgia

a context caroms from the contours

and every border could not at first

be seen or felt to be

is now revealed as environment Georgia

to fetter the setting it occupies

and this becomes known as the world Georgia

or at least as one world

among possible worlds

however exhausted the term Georgia

in company or alone

and whether those possible worlds Georgia

be many

or only

my own

I call you Georgia

in the fissure of you

the flocked light and parataxis of you

are you going to come before the darkness shuck its dark

mercury Georgia

musket ball Georgia

unlessless Georgia

for the blossoms Georgia

the night is leaded with cheap perfume

I won't sleep Georgia

I'll wait up

for Sandrine

ARROW'S SHADOW

gauntwater and brittlewhite

a word
among the oxygen
shriven and shirred in a canticle
nowise its own and nothing to do with
the porticos of its origin
the para-
noise
the wane
and bowstrung toward the weather's intermezzo

a palimpsest of shatters
letting the limit appear

as if a storm opened up in the palm house
and were caught on camera, on cardioid mic
trysting the chandeliers of sateen
of folding fan and chloro-
phyll

thunder's faint fac-
simile and sigil
woofing under trefoil vaults
its pinnate fronds a coiffed
a viridian ocean

still life with eau-de-nil
with zerologue
with motion

periph-
eries are the centers of other things

by modemsong and binaural breath, lip-
synced and bootlegged along a scrim-
shaw property fence

the contrail of a porph-
yry star slipping out of range

by lumière's silkscreen paraph-
rase, from a lemongrass leak in the sky

while earth and the sun in reel-to-reel

type-
set as an um-
laut, graf-
ted to a formica lake

sepia, gelatin print (in sotto
voce, in cablespeak)

the empress and the outcast

what ciph-
ered graf-
fiti they aero-
sol the walls with

o   o   o

the ana-
gram and gram
-mar of mar-
gins and mar-
igolds

multi-channel decoding inside the dusk

wind busks in the branches, wah-
wah pedals the lariat dark, a few leaves fall (pence from a poplar)
as the quicksilver virus and unzipped file
of sub-
ject and ob-
ject suspend their wetland lease

call sign
weak signal

lindens and larches
resolving anemic green

the exile, the extinction of a cloud
cued up and cranked fast forward on the hi-
fi mixing board and solar panels of a hill in late afternoon

anarch-
itecture's fraktur arch

(the heart is an ideogram)

compact discs in the cherry tree
if only the electric lines
if only the birds if
only the birds
sequencing in ultra-
sound and laying down a synco-
pated lead soprano track

if only the wrens as bottle rocket
as pinball eave to eave
the morning's gramophone and booting up

here, in the romper room, in the red-
light district of the lyric

the rose and the UV rays it reads are out-
sourced, hyper-
linked, filtered through the autobahns of abra-
cadabra
and idiolect

a search engine spinning its all-season radials

hot-wired, hi-
jacked by a para-
clete, some piece of the strange

working at the ed-
ges of the ed-
ge

a dyslexic, low-caliber dusk
jumper cabled by June and July
lit by a scherzo, a Janus-faced strobe

programmed on shuffle play
and repeat

off-
keying the exigent
the accidental snow
as buckshot, instant asbestos

in phenol red
in xerograph

calving the terraced draft of its crystal
atoll

while a trigger-happy copilot
side-
saddle and spin-
drift in his neon ejection seat
tumbles through the atmosphere at t-
minus 10
, 000 ′

maydaying remixed b-
sides
from a silent film soundtrack
to the tower

an emerald vamping italic on the skylight
filter, in the Polaroid rain

stapled in dog-eared fascicles

its whistled polyhymnia and Geiger counter counter-
currents, as sys-
tolic lightning toggles

between the horizon
and orison

chrysalis where a location meets locution

(the sound check, verb and reverb, the voiceover
-lap)

the river is a sibilant, sibyl-
line line

tildes where the tide belays

mur
-mur

a tear in the terra

and the trans-
literated dark
a shekel dropped among the asphodel

o   o   o

circuit breaker and breached circuit
stripping to a bar-
code beneath the whiskey tree

the fiber optic net-
work of mouth
on mouth on
mouth

broadband rainfall

fault line in the fault line

lowghosts listen
shuttered inside
the electri-
city-
scapes

of infra-red and china blue, distortion frazzling out-
put A, output B out
of whack

and a kite
rehearsing a cabaret

lens
kHz
lens

waking to interfaced, 5-channel snow
from a vascular cloud with its tracking askew

patched in and simulcast
on an iceberg cemetery
its apparencies of outside-
real sub-
junctive hoar
frost and haar

as if thought had thought of its own
riffing on paraf-
fin darknesses, kimono-colored fields
(the abstract blizzard with a sarabande pulse
a glacier lit by glam and frazil
by interior filament)

polar gust in contrap-
punto at –40°
a spun glass sonatina
for ic-
ic-
le and sci-
ntilla, viola da bracci-
o and voice

honed electrum or lamina blue
its first movement
movement deux

o   o   o

shadowword
aimed
shadowward

arrow of the under and over
canary yellow
chameleon green
arrow of the lisp and glottal stop

the fumed glass and fuel-
injected
(wind the arrow is fettered with, feather the arrow is fitted with)
arrow tuned a half-
step, a mis-
step sharp
by a navigational logarithm, a syntax lax in the draw

and the arrowhead polished to pure event, a marrow, cocaine blanc

and the bandwidth arrow, wavering

the garance arrow, a phylum of love
(silex traveling its secret vein
sent from other to other)

and the arrow of mock, trans-
lucent figuration

the joystick arrow

its milk tooth chipped
the aspirin and the firewall dart

inched off-course in the tourmaline snow
of a television receiver

and arrows that weave in rushing rain
thorn beloved of ballerinas
(its aura chromed with cesium leaf, wreathed with garlands of Joule
effect, of jonquil and jewel-
weed, detonating dental at the bull's
eye, the numb
-ered rings)
and the gallows arrow's flim-
flam, and how to flee the arrows of the frost and how
to freeze

o   o   o

on a wide-angle, agate sky
twilight shorts a fuse

cascara and liquidambar sputter
a pirate copied patois
in sequences of non sequitur
and inter-
rupted inter-
rupting shortwave intimacy

as the body and everything in and with-
out

(the lungs and their geodesic revisions
eyes developing thermal photos
high speed video-
stream
heart like a glass of chinon in the cochineal sun)

are seen as one sees
a hole
in a halogen lamp

fission and mute poly-
phony
each particle shearing to panicle

in the language / of the lifting up / and letting fall / of language

blue-
screened, air-
brushed

in x-band radar
Technicolor

its holo-
grammatic, centri-
petal petals
a cadastral map of the calyx
about to blossom
fugal

live weather on a live wire
virtual rainbow in real time
the lockstep and lurch of ground fog
of day-glo ablative
rap-
pelling off a rickety bridge
with raw silk rope and mercury
vapor
dubbed in a minor
key

what the runes
the ruins
say

in ballads of the scythe's blunt blade

o   o   o

traces a name driven south south
-west
as it ruses as it rises

and to stand beneath the loges
of the cloister carved of calc-
spar
at the introit and the end
of what has none

field recordings and micro-
fiche
of a world / in front of the / world behind / the world

(river running chicory

a sheriff wind
turning the teeth
of turbines along the ridge

nickel plated leaves in a drizzle

the chalcedony stain of a shanghaied star)

o   o   o

lower
limit language / upper limit
language

the archer unsheathes a rapture, nocks a scripture

at the turn of the season, verbena

at night, the ethics of night

minor limit elegy
major limit éloge

with a flight path for a project, a fuse
-lage as form

ruches our eyes with its arc, like a freight train of bl-
ackandbl-
ue and a fuckload of beautiful noise

the archer is an infantry of archers

is medium and pan-
demonium

is diadem

is none

the paper birches' leaves a blanched marquee

an arrow throws infinities of fissure

from upper level lower
us down (our air space and a-
topia, the horsetail inclusions
in our danced-out, demantoid
selves) to lower level levitate
on no

archer of the formula-
less
archer who measure our height

lower listen quiver / upper listen quill

in a mode of wrapped phen-
omen
-on
will flower
hearing your demo heart's r
-at-
at-
at
-at

o o o

tin-
tin-
nabulation

the tympanum a fan belt
whirring around the gear box and banging
a broken cymbal in the grief, the gravity sessions

a 2-stroke engine idyll cough and car-
buretor pentameter

the cylinders poppet a dead-
pan
a tin-
pan
pan
-egyric

dialect forged of phos
-phor
cadenza with a funny clutch
rearview mirror angled away from the sun

pain is the anti-lock skeleton
of a sudden
un-transparent to itself

(in extremis, in stereo, noise reduction off)

o   o   o

or the song of four red chambers
with a bellows to billow the embers

the sun's hier-
atic hier-
oglyph

the noun locked to a lo-jack

the verb glancing wireless

an an
-acrusis and colophon

of cantata barometrica, of Celsius madrigalia

anthem for cow bell and tuning fork
in a sonic tabernacle, a dial-up shuttlecock

a tourniquet to the motet
cacophony's mote
le mot

o   o   o

a fruit bat a cursor dragged by the dark
over ghost fonts silting the sower's lament
for altered window
ulterior wind

fidelity to a language / faithful to itself

speaks arthro-
scopic autumn gusts
and out-of-
focus alpenglow

the rouge, the rogue ascensions

over mountains as if cast in bonded salt

and the fiberglass boats and long goodbyes
the scarab word
the halfwayword
and a ping-ponging searchlight on the sound

and the geisha corolla, the harbor and buoys
midnightsewn, blatherskit-
tish, tallowed in scimitar blue

and the stained glass bones in their columns of coming to be
(the blood's sluggish jake-
leg and slalom through the structure)

and the least, the last thing said
as prefix
as praise
as variorum and opus
minimus

o   o   o

arrow

's shadow

flenses the armor before the flint can shirk

and passes through

o   o   o

in the beginning another beginning

low, annotated is-
lands

logic-board reef with its rib cage exposed

one by one, the estuary's scattered beacons blink

e-
clipse on a cadmium battery / splice

remote-control river

a chat room of gulls

let the blind, the liquid sentence, let the unfinished phrase

let the iris happen through its litanies
of ignite

whitecaps scribbled in capitals

japanimated trees

the arrow is toward a target gives it terror, gives it time

haunted, or hunted, does not touch is threaded by

takes its trace from the mark it would make
(sutures its serrated tip to the future)

if the negative arrow's itinerary, now
-here and next to now

the readymade sun, shadowdi-
stress, is pierced
at the spine of its spandrel

light molecules, nicked

knitted in the wake

eros as the arras

leukocytes'

formal

form
is the arrow's shaft, scrivened with the silhouette of its labor

air work, error work

in the field of the seeing of the field

o   o   o

oar stroke, key stroke

through a landscape up-
loaded
from seed vessel and CD-Rom

(the click clack of a stagecoach breeze
against a patio door

and the rotogravure of corrosion
scoring its handle)

as our romance running off-
road, the lingua off-
line

to the ergo-
nomic echo
-lalia hopscotching dis-
junc
-ture and junk

o   o   o

arrow hewn of a blowlamp

arrow hued in cage d'
amour

scrolls through bytes of helio dust

the sound-
bitten identikit sky
and 3-ring circus of the subject

the ghost-town nomen-
clature of a graph-
ite arrow's noumenon

the arrow as archipelago, screeds from logic to il-

from cryptogram and radiograph

to letter the arrow

litter the arrow

in il-
legibility, nohow and nil
in a no-fly-zone

a leaf's hidden aleph

phoneme and phonic fingerprint
rasping off the static line

the tremor at terminal velocity
is H_2O in a halter top
no stunt double no doubling back
(face first into gum arabic cirro, through bedouin alto
and cumulo blank)
with a rip cord in one hand
a coda in the other

abloom among the monographs of mid-
day and mid-
air
the unfurl of nylon
snaps to snare what's weight- and colorless

the chartreuse light a wayward word
's spinning jenny
and spinnaker

the daguerreotype moon a marquise-cut
spinel
called alias / and aileron / called margin-
alia

daybreak at 33 $^1/_3$

lul-
labied in a dumb-
waiter to wash the pell-mell etc
-etera
of our un-
un-
iform un-
iverse

· (cel-
luloid sleepers, a lol-
lipop stem, a wind-up whip-
poor-
will

making a racket of mala-
prop, of cel-
lo string and the rosined bow, of AM /
FM ephem-
era

in true-or-false false
-tto)

and the speak-
easy syl-
lables are pass-

word-
and penniless
a potter's field of hol-
low hal-
leluiahs

sentence under sentence

parole on parole

that language is silence's stop
-gap

its umbra and opening umbrel-
la
la

la

la

la

in memory of Gustaf Sobin (1935-2005)

STORM, LUSTRAL

UNEVENSONG

Blue as already the shoreline
is blurring   are you a
lakefront the question is
lacking   house with one
door with a corset of glass
its secret about

                to pass out of
earshot   faking its poker
face slurring its fall   apart
from white of which yellow
is part   sanding & sending
the slivers the hook the
ask and it shall

              open unto
cold blood & two
carat   how are you
overcast how is your hinge
brokedown the half note
in laudanum light :
frost at

         the window was
etched with such images
what if the dark does
not know to watch & what if
morning still biting its nails
bent with etcetera bent with
until   breathe

            a straight razor

notched like a tooth   to
break with the second the
third time around
a fretwork of shuteye at once
& awake   roomless for what got
wagered on the way

o   o   o

A carmine book   graphite red
book of rain will squall to smear
the first   the final page
& dusk at water's edge undress
the edge   a tantrum of fog
rehearses
             what used to be you :
birds filibuster a poplar
& stay the conductivity
of night   in this landscape
sampling another samples
others   wind with nothing to
stop or
             gear it down   not if
the half moon rig its pulley
roof to roof   sun make the
usual rounds   if let me have
my life it's what I have   if most
be fair in love & war but we   we
were never
                 : a piece of weak thread
& faraway thunder are work you
set your fever to   an oil
can   a threepenny nail   leaf
come in from the cold
or this space I call
for lack
          of a better word
                          me

o   o   o

Panning the river of where
he went for signs of where I
went   the gunmetal blue in
hemlock & water   rush grass
panic grass
                I can start
again can start again
: the moon is awaiting a
makeover   sun plays
satisfied with itself
& a speedboat
                    inscribing
its destiny on the dark
for don't know who
do not know why the wasp
the pebble   purslane &
clotbur
          seersucker
tree line   unable to
stay on the coast of a
concept a singular
thing that only happens
plural
        : hail   rain   wave
upon wave   someone
somebody else   & his
ragdoll figures of difference
with their foreign   faceless

god   that it runs

                runneth down

rattles to & fro

before running out

as a boy   at the end

of a party   will up &

leave his hat

           & satchel

behind   the sky eliding

from damask to cobalt

varicose over the barn

aluminum puddles &

zydeco light

            strewn around

the yard   open never open

enough in a winter at

one remove   while a pewter

cloud slipped its

drift & got

          untethered

for good

o   o   o

Rainstorm oiling a rusted
track   orange the farther
the fiery end   nonplussed & no
nonsense   refusing
to fold when the dealer
delays
            to sever each
premise go back on one's
will   consent to be riven
then breach one's consent :
why feather why do you
ice & erode   playing what's
meant by a
                color betrayed
nothing from nothing not
triage or whisper   night it got
busted got put back to pieces
tale of the splinter &
wind burn it got   frayed by
an absence that
                    rendered it seen
as sunlight can fissure
the arc of an echo   lured from
its ashes the violet
lamé   shadowless wave &
nerve pointing nowhere   filthy
& fucked up & bent
                    beyond fixing

even insomnia sawed off &
gray or tinted in gaillac or
black Sunday best   : flakjacket
heart will you walk a ways
backward empty of
anything

      other than snow

o   o   o

Anorexic & off-kilter   a snowflake
done brought the mountain
down   : reckons well what voice
will latch   beckoning
the dark   fathoms how a
halo catches fire
                    alike knows why
from now until never
if one be unslept to oneself
a kiss come wreck
this body & rearrange
our limbs   : December not
relaxed nor cut
                    the haywire of
its blear   but dragging
gaunt calligraphy over
the blue sharded glass
of being there   gone & left
a fraught   laconic poise
for none did see
                    : epilepsies
of sunlight marry the floor

o   o   o

Surrounded by piñon
& parasol pine   dog rose &
flowering plum & so far
ahead of ourselves I
                    no longer see us
where last we were seen
looking into oneway glass
unsure which side is clear :
mirror that sharps
                    if interrupted
mirror refuse to shatter
by the deadpan   ambient chord
of being alive with you
& almost alone
                    : why everything hangs
in the balance
even the balance

o   o   o

Although it is neither your
language nor mine   not
in the eyebright & not in
your name   no matter if
driftwood if pollen or cirrus
hauling their muted shadows
vex the shore   : although every
written must
                        other its author
a daybreak sonata   horizon
château   the private archives
of lakewind & loss   a claret tide
that's closer to me than my
self   : although wet japonica
as if by default   melissa or
ambergris   coltsfoot or burr
inhabiting
                        a single stroke of
sun   : give & forgive us
our tagalonglight
our fjords of crashing
through thaws of ourselves
analect & veer from an arsenic
sky   like a child who guards
a sand castle against
the afternoon
                        tapping a wrinkle
of salt water
telling the ocean to stop

[72]

o   o   o

By shot light & shadows of
overhear a took-off man
nearing the fence   the folds of
hop across its
                      talcum code
& piston the ditchwater of :
river level at curtain glass
junk awash on the bank
he swims ahead of an
                            undertow
stands for himself
if he had one   as a life that
partway happened leans
testing each
                      movement of
& clouds collapse in seigniories
gone mint   médoc   cassis
& not the forest
unseen for the trees
                            but I can't
see any trees   flying the
gravel or gravity of
organon & the opera of
clinging to the
                      negative
of a photograph
of the silhouette
of the dream of the dancing
of of

o   o   o

Believe the weather will
strain its back for
someone no longer & never
was there   for things that tremor
& things that hide &
things that lavish

    their future in
a flood   pastis green
of crossbow pine & indigo
trimming the veins   a bridge
that flexes like scissors below
& currents that waver
unbended untorn

    : in nil-nil time
turn without turning   don't let it
break let it rest let
it break   : red that unfreezes
a riot of red   may all my
arrows be written down in you

o   o   o

A tractor rasping its talon
along the dune
& dawn lifting saffron
blanched floss silk
off the sound
            the pupil
recite its conjugations of gold :
rape seed   paper lantern
mimosa   spider web
a steeplechase of cumulus
lithographs the bay at
                eventide
by this house composed
in aquarelle pine   plate glass
& ardoise   with pajama blue
shutters & samurai
ironwork
        a winter
garden to keep the winter out
but not out of sight :
recycling what murmurs
volt after volt
goodbye
        it's okay
goodbye
white flame in a white
fog in a windflower coming
to meet us

Notes

The book's epigraph is from "A Textbook of Poetry" 4, *The Heads of the Town Up to the Aether.*

"Georgia" is after Philippe Soupault. The poem also cites Maurice Blanchot, *L'Attente l'oubli*; Louis Zukofsky, *"A"*-22; William Carlos Williams, "The Descent of Winter" (12/2); Carson McCullers, "A Tree, a Rock, a Cloud"; and Charles Olson, *The Maximus Poems: Volume Three.*

Acknowledgments

"Georgia" is forthcoming as a limited-edition chapbook from Katalanché Press, edited by Dorothea Lasky and Michael Carr. Co-winner of the 1913 Prize, it also appeared, with short introductions by Peter Gizzi and Cole Swensen, in *1913: a journal of forms*, edited by Sandra Miller and Ben Doyle.

"Arrow's shadow" is due in the U.K. as a limited-edition book from Equipage, under the Cartalia Poetry Series editorship of Rod Mengham. The parts beginning "gauntwater and brittlewhite..." and "on a wide-angle, agate sky..." first appeared in *Miracle of Measure Ascendant: A Festschrift for Gustaf Sobin*, edited by Andrew Joron and myself (Talisman House, 2005). Other sections were published in, or on, *ars poetica, Boston Review, Coconut, First Intensity, Fourteen Hills, The Laurel Review, New American Writing, Talisman*, and *Van Gogh's Ear*. Several segments reappeared on-line at *Double Change*, alongside French translations by Sébastien Smirou, under the title "Wah-wah."

"Storm, lustral" first appeared on *Web Conjunctions*. The section beginning "Although it is neither your / language..." was included as "Unevensong" and, in Antoine Cazé's French translation, as "Inaccomplies : Chant dessus dessous," in the bilingual volume *Walt Whitman hom(m)age, 2005/1855* (2005), edited by Eric Athenot and Olivier Brossard and published jointly by Turtle Point Press, New York, and éditions joca seria, Nantes.

Thank you to the Ledig-Rowohlt Foundation, for its hospitality at Le Château de Lavigny International Writers Residence, Switzerland, where some of this book was written.

Further thanks to Dawn-Michelle Baude, Judith Bishop, Kevin Craft, Sika Fakambi, Ed Foster, Graham Foust, Forrest Gander, Peter Gizzi, Joshua

Harmon, Andrew Joron, Ed Pavlić, Jed Rasula, Joe Ross, Jennifer Schuberth, and Sébastien Smirou.

To Brian Henry, who watered and rewired these words.

My furthest to Sandrine — the nearest.

The Author

Andrew Zawacki is the author of two previous poetry books, *Anabranch* (Wesleyan) and *By Reason of Breakings* (Georgia), and of several chapbooks. His work has appeared in the anthologies *Legitimate Dangers: American Poets of the New Century* (Sarabande), *Walt Whitman hom(m)age, 2005/1855* (Turtle Point), *The Iowa Anthology of New American Poetries* (Iowa), and *Great American Prose Poems: From Poe to the Present* (Scribner). Coeditor of *Verse* and of *The Verse Book of Interviews* (Verse), he has published criticism in the *TLS*, *Boston Review*, *How2*, *Chicago Review*, *New German Critique*, *Australian Book Review*, *Open Letter*, *Religion and Literature*, and elsewhere in the U.S., Europe, and Australia. A former fellow of the Slovenian Writers' Association, he edited *Afterwards: Slovenian Writing 1945-1995* (White Pine). He teaches at the University of Georgia.